A Simplified Life

How to Achieve
Order and Calm
So You Can Reclaim
Time, Energy, and Control

Heather Rogers

First published by Heather Rogers

Printed in the United States of America

ISBN:

Library of Congress Control Number

Simply Organized
3365 Hutchinson Road
Cumming, Georgia 30040
www.simplyorganizedyou.com

To my mom and dad.
Thank you for your love, support, and infinite wisdom.

Acknowledgements

Thank you to my family, my husband, Tim, my friends, and my clients without whom I would not have been able to write this book. My father, Bill, gave me my entrepreneurial drive, and my mother, Tish, taught me everything I know about organizing. My brothers, Wil and Michael, have also been an inspiration for me. Together they have given me great advice.

Tim, you are the love of my life and have supported me through this crazy journey. Cathy, you have kept me sane throughout this process and helped me find my words. I also want to thank my Anitas; both have helped me immensely. There are so many other people in my life—friends, family, and clients—who have also been generous with their time and words of wisdom.

Finally, I'd like to thank those who took the time to read the first draft of this book: Cathy, Elizabeth, Anita, Wendy, and Michael. I truly appreciate your insight and suggestions.

Thank you all!

Contents

Introduction

If you're the person who constantly hears from others that you need to clean up, show up on time, or throw away some of that stuff, or if you consistently lose your keys and cell phone, have counters in your home or office that are covered with mail or papers, or you're constantly late, you're probably among the millions of people considered disorganized. Yes, millions, so you're not alone—not even close.

In my work as a professional organizer, I've noticed several common traits of disorganized people. (I should say common traits of most humans instead of "disorganized people" since this includes ninety-five percent of our population). They are usually running late, frazzled, overly tired, never have enough time to finish their tasks, and are embarrassed to ask for help. Sound familiar?

There's Nothing Wrong With You

If you see yourself in this description, I'm here to let you off the hook. There's nothing wrong with you. There's no perfect way to be in life. Everyone has their thing that they need to work on. So if yours is being more organized, you're in luck. There is an easy fix, and this book will show you how to attain it.

Being disorganized becomes a problem when you see negative patterns appearing in your life. For example, are you always losing track of your stuff: keys, phone, papers, and important contact information? Do you find yourself scrambling around the holidays? Are you always the last one to show up at a party or work function? For you, it may appear more subtly; you notice lots of unread emails, or your voicemail box gets full quickly. Perhaps your purse is in constant disarray, making it impossible to find anything. Are you missing appointments or showing up five to ten minutes late for activities?

Many people describe this feeling as being constantly overwhelmed. You may be very organized at work but can't seem to get it together at home, or vice versa. Sometimes disorganization shows up as avoidance. Is there one room in your home you hate going into? Perhaps your family dumps all miscellaneous stuff into the home office or basement, so you just keep the door closed. Do you avoid your email inbox because there are hundreds of un-answered emails? Many people turn to social media or television to escape their responsibilities because there are just too many to tackle.

What You'll Find in This Book

Being organized definitely has its benefits. It's not about being perfect or having the cleanest house. Being organized is about having control of your time, your energy, your space, and your life. This book will teach you how to get all these precious qualities and treasures back.

As you read, you'll discover a variety of benefits of being and staying organized. For many people, getting and staying organized is a challenge, and you'll learn about some of the personality types and the lifestyle triggers that can cause disorganization in your life. You'll also discover some of the blockages to getting organized, the costs of being disorganized, what it's like to get professional help, and how to maintain an organized life that works for you.

Most everyone—other than your Aunt Sally who everyone calls a "Neat Freak"—has some aspect of disorganization in their lives. (Remember those millions of disorganized people mentioned earlier?) Many don't know they need help. Some do, but they don't know what to do about it. Regardless of which group you're in, you'll learn some useful information and first (or next) steps to take.

You'll know you're ready for help getting organized because you've tried everything else and are ready to take the next step. You probably have no idea where to begin, so you never get past the first few minutes of trying. Hiring a professional organizer is one of the surest ways to get the results you want, to learn the critical insights needed to make a newer, more organized lifestyle work for you, and to maintain the organized spaces you've invested your time and sweat equity to create.

Who Am I to Be Writing This Book?

I'm a problem solver and a people person. I've been told I have a motivating effect on people, a gift for spatial planning, and a super-organized mind. I combine these traits in my work with clients at my company, Simply Organized, which I founded in 2011 to help people simplify their lives.

Working in my early teens and throughout my college years while attending the University of Georgia taught me some phenomenal skills I proudly use in my business today: customer service, risk management, balance, and time management. As my career evolved, I realized that I wanted more control over my days, my life, and my time. I wanted the opportunity to choose who I worked with and to do the kind of work I was passionate about.

When I was ready to find my true calling in life, I researched many different career paths and professions. "Professional Organizer" kept coming up over and over as a career I would be a good fit for. I used to watch *Clean Sweep* with Peter Walsh all the time, but I had not realized I could make a living helping people organize their lives. Being an organizer combines all of my passions and skills in a way that allows me to help take stress and pain away from others and enjoy doing it. What a gift!

After years of considering starting my own company and preparing for success, finally, I cut the cord, got off the hamster wheel, and leaped off the scariest cliff you can imagine—from being a full-time employee to being a full-time business owner. Many people thought I was crazy to give up a well-paying job, health insurance, a car allowance, paid expenses, and security to start a business. Now that I've run a successful business for over five years, I can honestly say it was the best decision I've ever made.

What Does It Mean to Be Organized?

Organizing is not about getting rid of everything you own; it's about making the things you use more easily accessible to you so you don't waste time and money. Like many people, you might feel overwhelmed in your home or office, or you might want more time in your day and less stress in your life. Being organized helps you have these things.

Taking a page from the David Letterman playbook, here are the top ten similarities among people I work with:

⑩ You have at least one area of your house or life that is in disarray.

⑨ You find it hard to ask for help (but everyone needs help).

⑧ Working alone to tackle your clutter is difficult and not much fun.

⑦ You need accountability. (Accountability is just as important as skills, motivation, and elbow grease.)

⑥ You decide when you are ready for a change. (No one can help you until you are ready and willing.)

⑤ You apologize because you're ashamed of your clutter.

④ You have at least one item in your home you're emotionally attached to.

③ You remark, "Wow, I've been looking everywhere for that," at least once, but usually many times, during organizing sessions.

② You want the perfect home. (Perfectionism is unattainable and should never be anyone's goal.)

① You already own at least one book about getting organized, often stashed under piles of items you need to organize.

Do any of these sound familiar to you? If so, read on to find the solution to help you achieve *A Simplified Life.*

1

What Happened?

"*I try to take one day at a time,*
but sometimes, several attack me at once."
~ *Ashleigh Brilliant*

How did it get like this? Most of my clients say they used to be organized. It's a lot easier to maintain a household when you have time, but all of a sudden life catches up with you and you have a job, kids, pets, family, and social obligations. That's if you have an uneventful life path with no special issues.

It's important to discuss all the reasons people are disorganized. Many people experience a major life change, such as marriage, divorce, moving, kids, death of a loved one, or job loss. When health crises, physical disabilities, disorders, or addictions enter the daily life ecosystem, what was once normal begins to take a new form. Areas of life that were once simple to manage and maintain suddenly become difficult to face. Paying bills on time, managing the daily mail (both snail mail and email), filing important papers, maintaining an appointment calendar, preparing balanced meals, keeping clothes and other items clean and orderly, and even getting enough sleep all become realities of the past.

The new normal begins to take shape, and for a while it seems manageable. Soon, confusion becomes common, forgetfulness sets in, time gets away from you, and life seems out of control. None of this happens overnight, and for most people, getting back to the way things used to be doesn't happen overnight either. It takes time and focus, and it usually takes help from a professional.

One of the most common life changes that affects home organization is marriage or remarriage.

So many people struggle with their own stuff; then they get married and the stuff doubles. I get called to help new families figure out how to make a new home by both combining the wanted and eliminating the excess.

I love many aspects of my career. In particular, I enjoy working with unique people and families. Two years ago, I had the pleasure of meeting a real-life "Brady Bunch" family. The couple had both been married, raised children, divorced, and lived in their own homes. When they decided to remarry, Karen brought her two children and Brent brought four of his own into their new home. Yes, there were three boys and three girls, but no Tiger or Alice in the mix.

Brent and Karen hired me just as they were merging their houses and families. My task was to assess their individual established homes, as well as their future shared home. My goal was to figure out what furniture should move with them, to come up with creative spatial planning to fit six kids (ages six to sixteen) into four bedrooms, and to set up a homework station for all six children that was not only organized but also had room for supplies and a flat tabletop to work on. Are you groaning just thinking about that task? Not me; this is the stuff I live for!

During our initial walk-through, I noticed the couple seemed on total opposite sides when it came to decision making. This is not uncommon in any relationship. Later in this book, I discuss the A and B personality types and how married couples are rarely the same. This means that you must have very clear communication and lots of compromise. (I know; that should be a four-letter word.)

Another issue that continued to come up was how they were going to raise the children in the same house with new rules, new schedules, and for some of them, new schools. Moving is very difficult for everyone, and you can imagine, with new step-parents and step-siblings, the move only added to the anxiety and stress.

After our walk-through of all three homes, I gave Karen and Brent a very detailed spreadsheet. Each room in the new home was noted with furniture placement, which kids would be sharing which rooms, and a separate sheet for the homework station that included tips for organizing assignments, managing a family calendar, and even a drop zone ideal for their incoming mail and paperwork.

Update: *The Brady Bunch is doing great. The kids have managed to all get along (for the most part) and even love sharing rooms. They are excelling at school and not driving their parents too crazy. It takes love, patience, planning, work, and consistency, but merging a family of eight can work. For this family, it was all worth it!*

Similar to marriage, divorce comes with its own disorganization issues. Not only does the couple have to divide their belongings, but they also have to accommodate the children in both their new homes. The kids usually need duplicates of clothing, food, sporting equipment, and electronics so they don't have to move everything they own every other week.

I worked with John, a divorced man, and his four teen-agers. His ex-wife still lived in town, but the kids were spending most of their time with their father (probably because he was very lenient). John was overworked and very stressed, trying to raise four kids on his own. My job was to get his large home ready to sell, since two of the four kids would be going to college and the family would not need such a large space.

You probably got a mental image as soon as I said a divorced man was living in a home with four teenagers, but allow me to paint a picture for you, just in case you have no idea what that might look like. The moment I walked into their beautiful home, I was hit with the pungent odor of cat litter boxes and dirty socks. The laundry room contained no less than thirty loads of unwashed clothes all piled up waiting for the nonexistent laundry fairy.

The countertops, coffee table, kids' bedrooms, and the entire basement floor were littered with dirty dishes and glasses. In between the biweekly maid service, the teens were not helping to clean up at all. The ex-wife had taken her beautiful artwork and tasteful furniture, so John and the kids were left with ripped couches and sports posters on the walls. I was so happy he called in my team for help.

After we decluttered all the closets, and the pantry, basement, and office (and got the kids to do their laundry), we staged the home with rented furniture and lovely art *and decor. We used an ozone machine, which sucks the oxygen out of the entire house, eliminating all odors, to tackle the cat odor, and the sock smell went away with the dirty laundry. A painter was hired to paint every room to cover the years of wear and to give the home a fresh update.*

After a month of hard work, John listed his home for well over the appraised value, and it sold quickly. Even though divorce and shared custody are challenging, you can always find help and hope for an exciting future.

What to Consider When Choosing Contractors

When you need help with home repairs, finding reputable contractors, handymen, painters, plumbers, or electricians can be a headache. Using a trusted company that already has connections with qualified providers can be a lifesaver. There is never a convenient time for things to break in, on, or around your home, but when they do, most homeowners, do not want to spend time searching online or flipping through directories to find the right contractors for the job. And you don't want to wind up with poor workmanship or an incomplete project.

So, how do you get it done right the first time, and save yourself some time, money, and headache? Hire only insured providers who have been vetted by a third party. Also, get a detailed written estimate prior to starting the project. Estimates should be specific about the scope of the project, materials to be used (including colors or brands), clean up, expected completion date, and payment schedule. Legitimate contractors will happily create the written estimate because it protects them as well. Communicate in writing and summarize phone conversations via a follow-up email to ensure you and the contractor are on the same page. Review all work to ensure it is completed to your satisfaction prior to making the final payment.

Imagine making one phone call and finding a qualified, reputable contractor for any home repair need you have. No more searching the Yellow Pages. No more hopeful calls to friends. No more Facebook blasts. No more reading reviews, hoping they're real. Get trusted contractors quickly and easily with HOCOA—The Home Repair Network—and get your project off to a great start. HOCOA provides you with insured, qualified contractors for all your home repair, maintenance, and improvement needs.

Check us out at www.HomeRepairNetwork.com

Stranded Stella

Stella is a good example of the many changes we experience that can throw us for a loop. She experienced her husband's death, her own failing eyesight, and a move all in one year.

Stella had lived in her lovely home with her husband for sixty-five years while raising three children. When I met her, Stella's husband had been deceased for a little over one year. Stella was mentally sharp, and physically she was quite fit, except for her eyesight. She was unable to drive herself and depended on neighbors and friends to take her on errands. During their long and happy marriage, Stella and her husband had traveled the world together, taking hundreds of trips, including several cruises. Every trip they went on, she would bring back a memento (or two, or a dozen). She was an avid collector of everything from The Lion King trading cards to Coca-Cola bottles to Steiff teddy bears and outfits for every occasion. Needless to say, her house was full of memories.

I was hired to help move Stella from her 2,000-square-foot home to a 400-square-foot apartment in an assisted living facility. Since she had not moved in several decades, she was understandably anxious.

We had some fun moments, like when I found more than seventy bars of used Dove soap she kept in her dresser drawers. This, she explained, was her unique clothes-freshening system. We laughed together at the thousands of

"You could win millions of dollars" letters she had received from Ed McMahon over the years and stuffed into her kitchen cabinets. Her rationalization, like that of many of my clients, was "I didn't know if I should throw it all away."

On moving day, we got Stella settled at a table with some of her peers at her new home. I unpacked her clothes, medication, toiletries, towels, and photos. Yes, the teddy bears came too. (To find out how many she brought with her, go to page 125). When she got into her new apartment, her bed was made and all of her dresser drawers were labeled so she could find her new clothes easily. In her living room, she finally got to use the glass-top bear table her husband always hated.

As we sat in the dining room after lunch, she said, "I think I'm going to be happy here." The look of relief and peace on her face was priceless. "They have so much good food and so many nice people," she added. And finally she said with a smile, "I'm looking forward to trading in my daily habit of wearing a housecoat and getting back into the beautiful dresses I used to wear on all those cruise ships."

At the start of this project, Stella thought she would never be happy anywhere except in her own home. In one month's time, we helped Stella move to her new place, held a successful estate sale, cleaned her home, and prepared it for sale. Stella was thrilled when the buyers told her they wanted to keep the house just as it was.

Another common cause of clutter among kids and adults is attention deficit disorder or ADD. I have helped many clients over the years with both diagnosed and undiagnosed attention deficit disorder, and I have learned that people who have a deficit in attention usually have a surplus in creativity, intelligence, and sensitivity.

According to Barkley, et. al., in a 2002 International Consensus Statement on Attention Deficit Hyperactivity Disorder (ADHD), "ADHD is nobody's fault. ADHD is NOT caused by moral failure, poor parenting, family problems, poor teachers or schools, too much TV, food allergies, or excess sugar. Instead, research shows that ADHD is both highly genetic (with the majority of ADHD cases having a genetic component), and a brain-based disorder (with the symptoms of ADHD linked to many specific brain areas)."[1]

Artistic Allison

Allison, one of my first clients, wanted her art room organized; she had a full-time job and painted in her spare time. Our first meeting took two hours, and we got nothing accomplished because she was whizzing around, frantically trying to explain what she used each room for, how she painted, the importance of light in her art room, canvas storage, why she kept every magazine she'd ever received, why she kept all of her art notebooks, areas she'd been avoiding, failed relationships, deaths, divorces, and so on.

---

1 R. Barkley et al., International Consensus Statement on Attention Deficit Hyperactivity Disorder (ADHD). Reprinted from Clinical Child and Family Psychology Review, Vol. 7, No. 1, March 2004.

Based upon her energy, I assumed Allison might have attention deficit disorder, and I appreciated her telling me that she did. In order for us to help, it's important for our clients to trust us. Allison trusted me with her personal history, which helped me come up with a plan to make the most of our sessions together.

Allison and I discussed how we could get the most focused time during our sessions. In my experience working with clients with ADD, I've learned that it's very important to remove distractions, like phones or televisions, while working. Another helpful practice is to use very strictly timed sessions. I would give Allison a twenty-minute task and set a timer. Each task had a specific beginning, ending, and goal to achieve. For example, for twenty minutes, Allison would go through a set of paintbrushes to decide which ones she wanted to keep. After we had all the brushes she wanted, we then sorted them by type (watercolor, oil, etc.). Allison and I worked on each area of the room this way, and while she was taking a five-minute break between sessions, I would put away the brushes and place the discarded items into bins to donate or trash.

Update: *After five three-hour organizing sessions, we completely organized Allison's art room and canvas storage room. The work we did enabled her to get inspired by her art again. She paints on a regular basis and has not gone back to her chaotic ways. Since we set up an organized system for her, where she can find all of her supplies easily and put them back in their place each time she uses them, Allison has no problems maintaining the organization in her art room.*

This is what Allison shared about her experience working with Simply Organized:

"I marvel at how empty that room looks now, which is a good thing! Before it looked so crowded and cluttered and crammed with stuff. Things were strewn all over the floor! I love the way the studio and the shop look now—just amazing! I will have a place for everything now."

Slow & Steady Stacey

Stacey is one of my typical (everyday) clients. Throughout the book, you'll read snapshots of my work with Stacey and follow her progress to create and maintain order and calm in her life.

Sometimes a lack of knowledge or skill when it comes to organization causes the clutter. Most people just don't know how to get started, or they can't seem to complete the process. Many of our clients throw everything into bags or bins to deal with later and then forget about it.

Then there are people who know what to do but don't have the time to get organized. A busy life keeps them from having the time to address the problem. Sometimes the clutter has grown to the point where they're overwhelmed. Being disorganized and living in chaos adds stress to their already hectic lives.

Stacey came to me with several typical issues: lack of time, lack of focus, and lack of skill in organizing. What she had plenty of was intelligence, heart, and stuff.

I see some clients one time; others I work with until their project is finished. I also have clients who prefer a long-term maintenance approach. These clients are the ones who can set long-term goals and work steadily to achieve them. They set appropriate expectations and know they will continue to need help from time to time to maintain their orderly space.

Stacey was one of my maintenance clients. She knew herself well enough to schedule me once per quarter. If she tried to solve all of her problems in a day or a week, it would totally overwhelm her. Her whole house needed attention, so we decided to focus on one room per session.

Everyone has their thing, or sometimes things, and Stacey's were books and music. She was very open and honest about what she would and would not be willing to part with in her home. While she was willing to donate tons of clothing, dishes, and electronics, there was no way she would get rid of a book or CD.

This information is actually very helpful to organizers. Knowing what you will and will not part with helps me understand the boundaries we are working with. I never go into someone's home to throw stuff away, and I like to make that clear. My goal is to create a system that works for each individual client so they can find what they need when they need it.

Stacey's favorite sentence was: "Make it go away." Over the years, it has become music to my ears to hear clients say those words. Not only does it tell me they are motivated, but I know if I make it go away for them, I've done my job. As a professional organizer, I'm a problem solver, and this is an easy problem to solve.

Over the course of this book, we will check in on Stacey to see how, with my help, she got organized.

Another cause of disorganization is shopping addiction. Oftentimes, people recovering from addictions (such as alcoholism or food issues) try to fill the void with something else. Sometimes this manifests in shopping; buying stuff makes them feel better even if they know they don't need the item. Unfortunately, the consequence to overbuying is clutter. Physical clutter always becomes emotional clutter, so shopping is not the best solution.

According to a study by CreditDonkey.com, "Nearly 11 percent of those polled said they frequently shop to improve their mood, 24.4 percent admitted they have items in their closets that are still in shopping bags or have price tags, and 18 percent said they often purchase items that they don't need or didn't plan to buy when they set out to shop."[2]

Any of these causes of disorganization might sound familiar to you. If you find that you fit into any of these categories, and if you've ever tried getting organized on your own but failed, you might benefit from using the expertise of a professional organizer.

---

2 Charles Tran, "Survey: Shopping Addiction Statistics," CreditDonkey.
   November 13, 2013. Accessed April 5, 2016.
   https://www.creditdonkey.com/shopping-addiction.html

Hiring a professional organizer is one of the surest ways to get the results you want, to learn the critical insights needed to make a more organized lifestyle work for you, and to maintain and enjoy the organization a professional helps you create.

2

Cha-Ching

"One's own self or material goods, which has more worth? Loss (of self) or possession (of goods), which is the greater evil? He who loves most spends most. He who hoards much loses much."

~ Lao Tse

You might find it difficult to see all of the ways being disorganized affects your life. For most people, there are four primary ways disorganization becomes costly:

- Time
- Money
- Focus and Effectiveness
- Stress

Time

When you're in the midst of trying to balance the home, work, and social aspects of life, things can get lost and downright mixed up. Placing an item you use often in a spot that seems convenient at the time can result in confusion when you search for it later, in the place where you know it belongs, but can't find it there. Busyness, rushing, and jam-packed schedules, in addition to emergencies and other unplanned events, can throw you for a loop, causing your best intentions for being organized to become a fleeting thought.

As you've likely experienced, there just don't seem to be enough hours in the day to get everything done, but do you realize how much time you waste looking for stuff?

According to *The Daily Mail*, "Over the course of our lifetime, we will spend a total of 3,680 hours or 153 days searching for misplaced items. The research found we lose up to nine items every day, or 198,743 in a lifetime. Phones, keys, sunglasses, and paperwork top the list."[3]

---

3 "Lost Something Already? Misplaced items cost us ten minutes a day," *The Daily Mail*. March 20, 2012. Accessed April 5, 2016.
http://www.dailymail.co.uk/news/article-2117987/Lost-today-Misplaced-items-cost-minutes-day.html

The time spent (or lost) searching for these items can never be regained. Imagine how this lost time could be better spent leaving early to arrive at your intended destination on time and less frazzled, enjoying quality time with loved ones, generating revenue in your business, relaxing, exercising, thinking, or creating a masterpiece. Wouldn't you rather spend (or invest) your valuable 3,680 hours doing these activities instead of searching for misplaced items?

Another time-related cost of disorganization is being late. It not only costs you financially—like when you get a fine for filing your taxes late—but it can also be embarrassing. If you consistently find yourself apologizing for your tardiness or asking for extensions on projects because you've missed deadlines and appointments, the time cost is obvious to those around you, which is a poor reflection on your reputation and effectiveness. You are also wasting other people's time when you're late. You don't like waiting for the doctor or hairdresser when you have a scheduled appointment, and your friends and colleagues don't like waiting on you either. When you are late, you disrespect and devalue the other person's time.

Lateness often creates a snowball effect. You may start your day only being five or ten minutes late, which doesn't seem like a big deal. That tardiness follows you to your other appointments all day long. By the end of the day, if you've had five appointments, you show up to your last appointment thirty to sixty minutes late. Each late appointment causes the other parties involved to be late to the rest of their appointments too, so your five to ten minutes have now caused several hours of lost time to others.

It is important to make the most of the time you have. Here are some helpful tips to do so:

If you are going to multitask, do one physical and one mental activity at a time. Don't talk on the phone and email at the same time; you could wind up accidentally sending your whole company something inappropriate. What you might be able to do is talk on the phone and fold laundry or unload the dishwasher.

Another fairly safe multitasking activity is cleaning out your car while pumping your gas. The importance of "uni-tasking" becomes clear when you take a break from multi-tasking and allow your mind to focus on just one thing. For example, you could take a walk with your cell phone off or drive your car in silence. Your brain needs these brief breaks from all of the noise. It helps you relax, whether you know it or not.

Money

Time is not the only cost of disorganization. Money is a tangible cost of being disorganized. Stephanie Winston, author of *The Organized Executive*, estimates "A manager loses 1 hour per day to disorder, costing the business up to $4,000/yr (if earning $35,000/yr—or $8,125/yr at $65,000)."[4] Money in the workplace is lost when you buy office supplies multiple times because you can't find the ones you purchased last month. You also miss important deadlines, which means *excess fees* and lost cost savings from missed "early bird" deals.

---

4 Stephanie Winston, *The Organized Executive* (New York: Warner, 1983).

This cost is amplified if you charge by the hour. Think of how many hours you could have been paid for instead of wasting that valuable time on other things caused by disorganization. Remember the snowball effect mentioned in relationship to time? If time equates to money, you have now lost a lot of both.

People also lose money due to lack of follow-up with prospects and because of missed appointments. Imagine you charge by the hour for the services you provide, but you forget to log your time. You and your company could lose hundreds of thousands of dollars due to this forgetfulness. Not only that, the stress and fear of losing your job could become a daily issue. Establishing a simple process, such as setting alarms or creating routines, could rectify this problem.

Disorganization drains your pocketbook at home as well as at work. Quick! How many pairs of scissors have you bought? People who are disorganized purchase household items again and again because they can't find them. And how many trips do you make to the grocery store or other places because you didn't make a list or you forgot something? That is gas money and time being wasted.

Focus and Effectiveness

New studies have proven that no one can multitask well. According to a 2014 article, by Vanessa Loder, in *Forbes Magazine*, "Researchers at the Institute of Psychiatry at the University of London studied 1,100 workers at a British company and found that multitasking with electronic media caused a greater decrease in IQ than smoking pot or losing a night's sleep."[5]

When you are disorganized, you can't focus on any one thing well. You are probably distracted by the number of items on your to-do list combined with losing and looking for things. It's hard to be effective at your job or in your home life with everything pulling you in so many different directions.

You might not realize that technology, while making your life easier, causes huge distractions in your day. If you can remember the time before cell phones or email, or email on your cell phone, you probably recall that your life seemed quieter or easier back then. A family could eat a meal together and talk about their day without bells, dings, and buzzes going off every few minutes. This type of interruption causes even more disorganization. It takes focus and attention to work on one task to finish it. It's hard to focus with all of the technological distractions we have now.

Stress

In all of the areas mentioned—time, money, focus and effectiveness—there is a direct correlation to stress. Cluttered spaces also cause stress. It has been proven that physical clutter leads to mental clutter, which manifests as anxiety, feeling overwhelmed, and being really stressed out.

---

5 Vanessa Loder, "Why Multi-Tasking Is Worse Than Marijuana For Your IQ," Forbes.com, June 11, 2014. Accessed March 30, 2016, http://www.forbes.com/sites/vanessaloder/2014/06/11/why-multi-tasking-is-worse-than-marijuana-for-your-iq/#2bb50e964e51.

An article on *HuffPost Home* in May 2013, titled "Home Organization Is Major Source Of Stress For Americans, Survey Finds," explains that "Among all those who experienced some level of stress about home organization, nearly a third expressed being very or extremely stressed by their homes. And it wasn't just a stressor for women: 81 percent of men and 87 percent of women reported experiencing anxiety over home upkeep."[6]

Living in a cluttered home also costs you space (physically and mentally). Any clutter in your home also tends to cause guilt, denial, shame, and stress, which are impossible to put a price on. Having a garage full of stuff, for example, may not seem like a big deal, but over time it subconsciously causes you unnecessary anxiety. This is usually the first space you see when you get home and the last place you see when you leave for work each day.

You now know that there are numerous benefits to organization, such as having control of your time, your energy, your space, and your life. In addition to control, less stress, and more time, I hope you also see one of the big benefits to being organized is removing unnecessary costs, both financially and personally.

It's difficult to put into words the feelings my clients experience after living with clutter for so long and then having it gone. Many have said things like: "I have so much more free time now," "My kids are cleaning up without me nagging them," and my favorite, "We love spending time in our home again." As you read the next

---

6 Carolyn Gregoire, "Home Organization Is Major Source Of Stress For Americans, Survey Finds," The Huffington Post, May 22, 2013. Accessed March 30, 2016, http://www.huffingtonpost.com/2013/05/22/home-organization-stress-survey_n_3308575.html.

few chapters, you will see the multiple ways getting and staying organized will help you at home and at work, both mentally and physically.

Later in this book, you'll learn several strategies and systems to overcome the costs of disorganization. The tips and tools provided will save you time and money.

3

Help
Me!

*"Asking for help is not a sign of weakness,
it is a reach of caring. Allowing others to help you
is a gift, not a burden."*
~ Agingcaregivers.com

Many people are afraid to admit they need help, and most have a very hard time asking for it. This comes from a need to be seen as strong and independent. The predominant thought seems to be: *If I don't ask for anything, I have everything under control, and others will see me as having my act together.*

As human beings, we all have an ego and pride that often cause us to believe we can solve our own problems, all alone, all the time. We live in a very independent era and society. The saying "It takes a village" gets said but not used. Only one generation lives in each home now, when we used to have grandparents living with us to help out. Swallow your pride and ask for help.

When you try to take on too many tasks yourself, you wind up overwhelmed, not achieving your goals, and frustrated. With just a little guidance and motivation from an organizer, you can check off that long list of to-do items. Most people don't know where to begin. You begin by picking up the phone and asking for help.

Dapper Dan

I have helped many senior clients downsize. Although it's never an easy experience, it's always rewarding. Dan was a widowed eighty-eight-year-old man living in a very large home when I met him. My favorite part of working with older people is listening to their stories. They have lived such interesting, rich lives, and they love to tell us about it. Dan was no exception. In fact, I'm pretty sure he had already lived about four lifetimes in his eighty-eight years.

Dan was an architect, musician, sculptor, painter, tennis pro, golfer, husband, and great neighbor. There are many things members of "the Greatest Generation" have in common, and one of them is fierce independence. Dan had moved over twenty times in his life and never hired packers or movers. Also, he may have seen asking for help as a sign of weakness. After several weeks of unsuccessfully trying all by himself to pack and clean up for this next big move to an apartment, his friend and neighbor convinced him to let us help him.

Dan had been in his home for more than twenty-five years. It was over 6,000 square feet, and although it was not packed with stuff, it held many of his precious memories. Like most people of a certain age, Dan was beginning to have trouble going up and down all the stairs. He had experienced a couple of falls and could not hear very well. Although he still drove, shopped, cooked, and golfed, it was time for him to move into a smaller place, where someone would look in on him from time to time. He chose a two-bedroom apartment in an independent living facility not far from his home. Our job was to pack him up, unpack him in his new place, and get the former home ready to list.

At first, Dan was reluctant to let go of his treasures. He had been a fashion model and wanted to keep most of the clothes from sixty years prior. He also had a love of chairs. (Guess how many he took with him. See page 125 for the answer). The most valuable items Dan wanted to take with *him, apart from the clothes and chairs, were his books. Now, I consider myself a book hoarder, but my collection pales in comparison to Dan's. He left quite a few for the estate sale, but we packed up at least a thousand books to take to his new apartment. After we moved him and got him unpacked in his new place, we went to work on his former home. We had a successful estate sale, followed by donation and clean-out and some repairs.*

__Update:__ Fast forward, and Dan loves his new apartment. He is surrounded by his favorite things, doesn't worry about falling on the stairs anymore, and has quite a few lovely ladies interested in getting to know all about his fascinating life. We still talk from time to time, and he's always so appreciative of all of the help we were able to give him during his stressful move.

Advance Preparation Is Useful in Planning a Smooth Move

Moving is said to be the third most stressful life experience individuals will face, after death and divorce. But there are a few ways to make moving a stress-free experience for you and your family.

Success begins with planning. Choose a non-peak move time, such as during the fall. Start well in advance of the move by decluttering your home and packing a box or two every day to make the task more manageable.

Selecting a trusted moving company is critical to ensuring you have the manpower and equipment you will need for your move. Your moving company should not only be reputable, with a good track record, but also provide hassle-free service that is cost effective for you.

At Atlanta Peach Movers, we have carefully crafted inventories and formulas to estimate moves based on years of experience with thousands of moves under our belts. We take into account your personal situation, the logistics of your particular location, and other factors that may help us recommend the crew size and equipment that are right for your move.

To learn more about our approach to helping you experience a stress-free, smooth move, visit us at www.AtlPeachMovers.com.

Asking for help can be hard, but it can make getting and staying organized so much easier. Do you need an organizer to help you take control of your life? Remember that the role of a professional organizer is not to throw away all of your cherished possessions, to sift through your personal items, to chastise and shame you, or to analyze or diagnose. The role of a professional organizer is to help you realize your goals by decluttering, creating systems, and making you accountable to maintain the changes you've made.

Check out this chart to see if hiring an organizer is right for you.

Should You Hire a Professional Organizer?

A Professional Organizer Could Be the Answer for You

There are over twenty specialties in the organizing industry, including financial organizers, photo organizers, and those who specialize in hoarders, students, moving, and more. I am what's called a generalist, although I like the title "Problem Solver Extraordinaire." Other terms for my focus as an organizer include:

Solutions Expert, Order Restorer, Resolution Guru, Chaos Controller, Calm Coordinator, Dilemma Demolisher, Discombobulation Destroyer, Excuses Executioner, Neat Freak, Nonsense Ninja, Squasher of Sadness, Wish Fulfiller, and your Giver of Glee.

Simply put, I examine your space, help you identify and address the core challenges, and develop a system to help you function efficiently in your life. I can do just about any type of organizing needed, from making sense of your cluttered closets, cabinets, and drawers to helping you experience a stress-free move to downsizing, organizing for time management, and even preparing for new family members (such as a new baby, elder, returning college student, or holiday guests).

Each organizer brings a unique history and set of skills to the table. If we figure out I'm not the right fit for you, or there is a problem I think is better solved by someone else, I can probably find the most helpful organizer for you.

Before hiring a professional organizer, ask yourself these questions:

- Do I like to work alone or in a team?

- Can I focus for several hours, or do I like shorter sessions?
- Do my goals include multiple spaces or just one focused room (baby's room, office, closet, etc.)?
- Do I need help at home and at work?
- Would I also like help with time management?
- Do I need a personal assistant who comes weekly or bi-weekly?
- Do I need any project management work done, like hiring contractors?
- Do I need help packing or unpacking for a move?
- Do I need help with downsizing?
- Do I need help with my small business finances, bookkeeping, or QuickBooks?
- Does my child with ADD need help organizing his or her schoolwork?

How you answered the questions above will let you know if you need a specialist. The right organizer can help you with all of the above-mentioned areas.

Are you still a little nervous or reluctant about the idea of hiring an organizer? The next few chapters will take some of the mystery out of the organizing process to make you feel more comfortable with the concept and help you understand what an organizer can do for you.

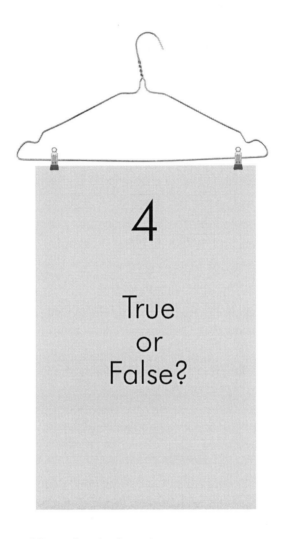

4

True
or
False?

"Give thanks for what you are now,
and keep fighting for what you
want to be tomorrow."
~ Fernanda Miramontes Landeros

I liken my profession to that of a personal trainer. You could exercise by yourself, but you will see better results working with a trainer who provides knowledge, motivation, and accountability. As a professional organizer, I bring specific skills and knowledge to your organizing project to help make the most of your space and develop a process that works best to organize your home or office. However, the added service of helping you get through the rough patches, such as wanting to give up, along with keeping you working towards your goals, are the reasons we see success when in the past you may have experienced failure.

Most people have never worked with a professional organizer, so a lot of misconceptions about the process exist. The below chart helps separate fact from fiction.

Myth vs. Truth

Myth	Truth
Organizers keep a perfectly clean and organized home 100% of the time.	Organizers are human just like you. Perfection is un-attainable.
You have to be wealthy to afford an organizer.	Most people who use professional organizers are middle class and have saved and budgeted for these services to make their lives easier. Using an organizer is not only affordable, but can save you time and money in the long run.

Myth	Truth
People who hire professional organizers are hoarders.	People with the tendency to hoard are few and far between. They usually have a life-long mental issue that is causing the hoarding.
You can go to the organizing store, spend a bunch of money, and you will suddenly become organized.	Lots of people have bins, pretty boxes, and really cool file trays that do not make their problems go away. Getting and staying organized usually doesn't cost a ton of money. It requires time, goal setting, focus, and elbow grease.
You have to organize or clean before the organizer shows up.	By not cleaning up first, you allow the organizer to see the way your home or business looks every day. This way he or she knows what your needs are and can put together a more efficient system for you.
You have to change who you are to be an organized person.	Living in a cluttered environment doesn't make you a mess as a person. The same goes for the "always neat and on time" people in your life; they may have the most stuff hidden behind their closed doors.

The following tips will not only help you if you ever hire an organizer, but will help you organize yourself as well.

Shop last. You can't know what you will need until after you organize the space. This is why spending a thousand dollars at the store will not magically make you more organized. Seventy-five percent of my clients already have the items we need to get them organized.

Organizers are not psychic. We can sort through your papers, clothing, dishes, and other items, put them into like-item groups, make a pile we think you will discard, and even get a list of your clothing sizes so we can weed out the high school clothing that may lurk in the back of your closet. We cannot, however, make the assumption or decision to get rid of your stuff without asking you. I often work without my clients present, but I always need them at the end of a session or workweek to give me the final say-so. I hate to be the bearer of bad news, but you are going to have to make some decisions about your stuff and spend some time and energy to get organized. Don't worry; having an organizer makes this process much less painful and will actually save you time and money in the future.

Communication is the key to excellent results. Starting with a written goal and keeping the lines of communication open with your organizer during your sessions is extremely beneficial. The idea is to help make your home and office work for you, so you have to communicate when something is working and when it is not.

Organizers are problem solvers. Don't just say you want to own a fully functional pantry. Let us know what else is going on in your home and life; we may have the solutions. Some organizers are also home stagers, designers, and professional packers. Organizers have a large network of resources, especially if they are members of the National Association of Professional Organizers (NAPO).

Don't wait until the last minute. Most people tend to put off the tasks they do not want to do until the last minute. The earlier you call an organizer, the more likely you are to get the help you need. At least three times per year, I get a call from someone the day before they are moving. I have performed some pretty amazing organizer magic, but it caused lots of unnecessary stress to everyone involved. Just bite the bullet and call. Setting the appointment is the hardest part; the rest of the process is worth it. Like any other problem in life, the first step is admitting the problem, and then you can take action.

5

The
Rainbow
Unicorn

*"So many people wait around for the stars to align
to do what they're here to do. The perfect moment,
the perfect opportunity, the perfect state of being, etc.
Wake up! These states of perfection are myths.
They do not exist."*
~ Melchor Lim

No amount of intervention, pressure, or nagging can make you see your true self until you're ready. Change is hard but inevitable, and if you're as overwhelmed as most people, sometimes you just need a little help. Telling you something you need to hear—even in the kindest, most considerate tone possible—isn't enough to get you to make adjustments or improvements. You have to come to that conclusion yourself. Deciding you need help with organizing is a decision you must make on your own if you want to see lasting results. And when you're ready, we're here to help.

Getting and staying organized is a process that begins with the very first visit.

The First Visit—The Assessment

As a professional organizer, I will do an initial assessment before we get started on the real work. I need to see where the pain is so I can make it go away. I do this by helping you create a space where you can find everything easily so you feel more secure.

During the initial in-person assessment, you will explain what your challenges are, walk me through your unorganized space, and get an idea of the time and cost to complete your goals.

I also use the initial assessment to see the space in person because you may find it difficult to explain the situation. Some people use statements such as "I'm drowning in paper," or "My family says I'm a hoarder." Those who are in denial might say, "My wife needs your help," or "I can always find what I need, but the house is driving my family crazy."

Like most people, your description of your space might be exaggerated. Being able to see the space provides me with a good indication of how long the project will take and how motivated you are to get it done. If you're like most people, you might be embarrassed by this first visit. Sometimes people apologize for the mess or say things like "Don't freak out when you see this." Most people think they are the worst, but usually, they aren't.

Goal Setting

The first time I meet with my clients, I ask about their goals. What do you want your space to look like? When does this need to be finished? Tell me what would make your life easier. What room of your home do you avoid the most? Getting this information on the front end is invaluable. Not only can I learn why you need me, but I can also remind you of your goals throughout the process. Goal setting helps the organizer and the client stay focused and motivated.

Don't try to tackle your entire house at once. We work room by room and complete one project before moving on to the next, using the following steps to establish realistic, attainable goals.

Step 1. Decide what you want to use your space for
Is it currently an office that needs to be turned into the baby's room? Are you moving and your home needs to be decluttered to look more spacious? Do you want to see the floor of your bedroom again? Park one or two cars in your two-car garage? Find your food in your pantry before it expires? Be able to pay your bills on time?

Step 2. Determine your deadline and schedule

When we work with a client who has to move the following week, we use a completely different process than the one we use for someone who needs a system put into place for their family to use over a long period of time. Maybe you want to work on your time-management skills over a period of a year. You might have guests coming in town soon and need a room cleared up quickly. No matter what your deadline is, we can help you get the project done. Communicating your deadline helps you and us know how much time we have to finish the job.

Step 3. Prioritize

Some people are visual and need to see items out in the open or in clear bins. Others prefer not to see their stuff. If fashion is higher on your priority list than function, say so. Our team can come up with ways to store your items and make sure you know where to find them. To help you see the progress you've made, take a "before" photo of your space so you can compare it later.

Remember Stacey? Before her first session, we set goals and expectations. Her goals included priorities and time-lines. She wanted to start in her library and finish that room in our first session. She did not need the books organized

in alphabetical order or by author; she just wanted them all on shelves and in the same room. She needed me to purchase the shelves and have someone put them together for her. Stacey wanted to work quarterly with me, so we averaged four to six hours per session, once every few months. After each session, we assessed and planned for the next one. Stacey then told me her goals for each room so I could research some products for her and order what she liked.

After we come up with goals, a timeline, and priorities, we can focus on setting expectations. Remember that your house did not get this way overnight, so doing the work to get it the way you want it will take time and effort.

Expectations

Essentially, expectations are strong beliefs that something will happen or be the case in the future, or a belief that someone will or should achieve something. Client expectations vary. I'm not psychic, therefore, be prepared to tell me what your expectations are for our work together.

When I understand who you are and what you want—not just that you want an ideal space, but also what your dreams are for the future—I can be much more effective for you. Do you want to spend more time with your family? Can you one day see transitioning the toy room into the teen room? Would you love a reading nook for yourself? When you pull into the garage, does it make you stressed? Are your mail and papers piling up all over the counters? As we practice an open communication process, I am able to understand and help meet your expectations and can be a resource for you by developing creative solutions for your challenges.

Profiles in Client Expectations:

Sally wanted to get rid of her girls' excess clothing. She had six adopted daughters, and each of them had her own walk-in closet full of clothes. I assumed she would want all of the closets organized, but instead she just needed help deciding what to keep, sell, and donate. After I took away the discarded clothing, she considered the job a completed success. She did not need reorganization, just a little help. To find out how many dresses Sally donated, go to page 125.

Stacey expected every room of her house to be less cluttered and more organized. In fact, this was her ultimate goal. I expected this process to take much longer than it did. However, since Stacey had no emotional ties to her belongings (except her books and CDs), she was able to get rid of a high volume of clutter very quickly.

Jennifer needed her home staged before she listed it for sale. She assumed we would get rid of all of her furniture and replace it with brand new items. Her furniture was not only beautiful, it fit in her home perfectly and was neutral in color and pattern, so there was no need to add the cost and time to substitute all of her pieces with rented items. Despite her initial expectations, we helped her achieve her goal of a well-staged home, plus we saved her thousands of dollars.

A Saved Marriage

Occasionally, I get to work with couples, which is great because it takes a team to run a household. Almost every couple I meet includes one Type A and one Type B personality. This can make life together super interesting and fun. It can also be super frustrating and make you want to strangle your spouse. During my work with Tina and David, I found that they each needed someone outside of their relationship to validate their respective expectations and help them reach a compromise.

This was the second marriage for both Tina and David, and they were finding it difficult to merge their stuff and styles into their new house. I spoke to each of them about their vision and expectations for their shared home and for their office space in particular, since that was the area Tina initially contacted me about. Their goal for the office was to use it as a guest room and home office.

David had a collection of lighthouses and sailing art that did not mesh well with Tina's style, which was more contemporary. After some discussion, it turned out that Tina did not need to use the office at all, so it became the area to display David's art and to store his files. He now had his own man space. Tina decided to utilize another room in the home for her paperwork.

They did not have much clutter, but they needed a storage solution in their garage for holiday decorations and other items. We sorted through all of their items and made piles for donation, trash, and keep. The kept items were placed like with like and stored on their shelving in order of holidays, for the decorations, and in order of how often they needed to use other items, like gardening tools, paint, and automotive supplies.

When we finished, Tina and David were both very happy with the results. They had compromised on their use of space and their different styles and couldn't wait to start their new life together. In her testimonial, Tina said, "You saved our marriage."

Tina is the only client who has ever asked me to get something back from donation for her. To find out what that item was, turn to page 125.

What You Don't Need

You don't need to buy or have anything for the initial assessment or organizing session. I bring some supplies, like Post-it notes, markers, Ziploc storage bags, and garbage bags. Usually, the first part of the session involves physically sorting and mentally deciding. If you need a bin or shelving, I will let you know, and I'll either get it for you or tell you where to find it. Most of the time, you will have everything needed.

The Myth of Perfectionism

Perfection is essentially "the rainbow unicorn" because it doesn't exist. The world would be a better place if people would lower their expectations a smidge. Consider this; being organized means being able to find what you need, when you need it. Being organized is about enjoying your space and it not causing you anxiety. Having a photo-ready home is an unrealistic goal for most of us.

There is a website called Pinterest, where people post photos of beautiful homes, places, and things. This is akin to "regular" women comparing themselves to the latest supermodel on the cover of a magazine. Even if you had the same clothes and make-up, you'd probably never look like that supermodel. The same is true for your home. Instead of expecting us to help create the perfect home for you, let us make the most of your space and make it beautiful by your standards, not by anyone else's.

If you're living with clutter or some other form of disorganization, remember that it did not get this way overnight. You did not go to bed with an organized home and wake up to a cluttered mess. Do not expect it to disappear quickly. It would be great if you could snap your fingers or wiggle your nose and make the mess magically go away, but that's not possible. This process will take some time and attention. With help, you can achieve your goals.

No one is perfect—no one! After all, even Martha Stewart went to jail. She handled it in the classiest way possible, but the point is no one is perfect. Look inside yourself to find your core desires and values. They are probably more about making time for family than having your home featured on HGTV. Give yourself a break. Your goal for success at the end of your busy day could be to make the most of each glorious day, that your family is happy, or simply giving yourself a pat on the back because you got in a shower! No joke, every day, the first item on my father's to-do list is "Take a shower." Every day, my father gets to check at least one item off his list, and it makes him feel great. Set small, *attainable* goals for yourself and appreciate the little things.

Everyone Deserves a Junk Drawer

Since no one is perfect, and everyone has miscellaneous items that don't fit into one category, allow yourself a junk drawer or two. This is the go-to place for the items you use daily and don't want to run to another room in the house to get. In this drawer (usually located in the kitchen), you probably want to keep tape, rubber bands, paper clips, scissors, soy sauce packets, notepads, pens, batteries or charger cords, a multi-tool with a screwdriver and/or hammer, and maybe a few take-out menus. You probably keep most of your office supplies in your office and tools in your garage, but it's fine to keep what you need where you use it most, and that's usually in the junk drawer.

If you find your junk drawer growing into several or spilling onto the kitchen counters, it's time for a reorganization or purge. Throw away all the expired coupons, dead batteries, and keys that went to the house where you lived in 1967. Get a couple of drawer sorters to keep the items easy to find. Enjoy being human and relish in your junk drawer!

Positive
Penny

To achieve success with an organizer (or in any part of your life), you need to have the right attitude. Attack your goals with positivity, perseverance, and a sense of humor. Be ready to do this for yourself. If you are not, you will fail. Don't let anyone guilt you into organizing; it's a commitment, and you will succeed if you are ready, just like Penny did.

My most successful organizing jobs are due to the positive attitude and perseverance of my clients. My most positive client was Penny. She was the sweetest woman I had ever met. When she called me, she was already telling me all the reasons why she needed my help and the excuses as to how her home had gotten so bad. (Just so you know, all my clients say the same thing before I meet them. They're afraid that their house is the worst I've ever seen, but it never is.)

Not only was Penny's home lovely, so was she. After surgery for her rheumatoid arthritis, she had to live in the family room on the main floor of her three-story home, and she was unable to keep up with the day-to-day cleaning and organizing. I was tasked with cleaning out two closets and swapping her office in the basement with her guest room on the top floor. My team and I cleaned out her closets, sorted through ten years of paperwork, and set up a new system for storing her seasonal decorations. We then moved some furniture and even assembled a bed.

The most important part of this process was designing a system around Penny's needs. When you have physical challenges, you can arrange your space to fit your priorities. By moving her furniture around, we allowed Penny to stay in her home longer and to manage her day-to-day activities better, which was her key to independence.

Despite the pain she must have been in, I never heard one complaint from Penny the entire time. I begged her to take more breaks, but she was so determined to finish our project that she kept going, grinning through the pain. She was a hard worker and so positive that you would never know she suffered all day, every day.

That project was so successful that Penny hired us six months later to assist her company with a large redecorating project, including sorting and labeling more than two hundred framed pieces of artwork and clearing out the storage rooms that housed the pieces. Again, her positive attitude made the long days go by so fast.

Penny and I still work together. Every time I see her, she has a huge smile on her face and is always ready to get started. She knows something many people don't—the result is worth it! When we finish a room, she is so excited and appreciative. She also sleeps better knowing there is one less thing she has to worry about. We laugh through our sessions and truly enjoy the process of making her surroundings more peaceful and easier to navigate.

Penny is the most positive, hardest working person I know, so I'm always happy to work with her on projects. Her attitude and perseverance should be an example to all of us. When I hear myself complaining about a sore shoulder or a headache, I remember it's nothing compared to what so many other people experience. People like Penny are a good reminder to be grateful for every day and to keep a positive attitude.

9 Tips to Stay Positive During Big Projects

1 Set small, attainable goals.

2 Have a schedule to complete tasks and give yourself enough time.

3 Invite a friend or family member to join you for support and laughs.

4 Carve out a few hours each evening or weekend to focus on your project.

5 Play fun, upbeat music while you are working.

6 Check items off your list as you complete them.

7 Remind yourself you are doing great, and don't get disappointed when you don't finish immediately. Rome was not built in a day.

8 When you find yourself frustrated or upset, take a little break or switch gears to a different part of the space or project.

9 Reward yourself after you finish.

6

Ready,
Set,
Go

"If I must start somewhere, right here and now
is the best place imaginable."
~ Richelle E. Goodrich

Are you ready to begin? Probably not, but we are going to anyway. If you've been putting off organizing for a while, you may not be looking forward to tackling it. That is completely normal. Just like exercise, most people do not want to do it, but when you do, you feel so much better.

Motivated Molly

I have a very good friend who is also my client. She has been telling her mom for years she should also hire me. Her mom, Molly, was understandably scared of parting with her stuff and also concerned about anyone judging her living situation. Molly finally called me, and I met with both her and her daughter. Having a friend or family member with you can be comforting. The first thing she said to me was: "You're brave for coming into my home." I chuckled at being described as brave since I not only like the messes but think it's fun to tackle each client's challenges.

Molly told me she was nervous when I got there. I assured her that this was a common feeling and I would try to be gentle. Within one hour she had done a complete 180. She asked me to take hundreds of dolls for reselling. By the time we were done, she said, "I feel so good. Why didn't I call you sooner?"

We have now worked with her over four sessions. This woman is "on fire" motivated! She keeps telling us to take it away, and so we do. We donated six vanloads of china, coolers, small appliances, linens, clothes, and more. She was so excited to see the transformations in her home. She had her family over for the holidays and showed off her pantry and closets. (When is the last time you let someone see the inside of your storage closet?)

Preparing for Day One

If you have the urge to clean up your entire house before I get there, I urge you not to. I need to see what every day looks like in your home so I can solve your problems. If I can't see the issues, it's much more difficult to help.

Much like preparing for a big game, you, the athlete (client), must be ready for game day. Whether you realize it or not, you're likely to have some level of anxiety (positive or negative) about beginning the organizing process. That is perfectly normal. To help curb that anxiety, rather than clean up prior to your session, try these pregame activities:

- Get a good night's sleep. Don't stay up all night trying to clean your house for me or worrying about what we will be doing.
- Make sure you have blocked off the time from work and family for our session. Try to avoid leaving your sessions to take calls or send emails. This may not seem like a big deal since people are always multitasking, but it turns a five-minute break into a twenty-minute distraction, and it's hard to get refocused.
- Eliminate distractions, such as your cell phone, your children, or your pets (if they are needy). Turn your

cell phone on mute so you can focus all of your time
and energy on your project. Your children are wonderful beams of light and also huge time vortexes. If
your little ones are not likely to watch a movie for
two hours while you get work done, get someone to
take care of them for the time you are working on
your organizing project.

• Commit to staying focused. Although sessions may
be several hours, you should take short breaks from
time to time. Remember that we are providing a
service to you because you hired us to do so. If
carving out three to four hours of focused time isn't
possible for you, let us work independently and get
your input later. If you have difficulty with focus,
there are things you can do to help. You might find
that drinking coffee thirty minutes before you tackle
the project helps you stay focused. Perhaps breaking
up tasks into small time periods (twenty minutes
max) is more manageable than trying to tackle everything at once. Maybe playing upbeat music helps to
improve your mood and keeps the momentum
going. If you have physical disabilities or conditions,
such as rheumatoid arthritis, be sure to take lots of
breaks and sit as often as possible.

Who Should Be Involved?

There is no right or wrong answer to the question of who
should be involved in your organizing sessions. It all
depends on your goals, your focus, your timeline, and
whether the end result will affect others. If you have ever
wondered if your children or spouse should be involved

with your organizing sessions, here is a short quiz to help you answer that question.

Are you working in their space?	☐ Yes	☐ No
Do you need them to make decisions about what stays and what goes?	☐ Yes	☐ No
If it's your child, will he or she be able to make a decision, or is it best that your child is not present?	☐ Yes	☐ No
Do they have the same goals as you?	☐ Yes	☐ No
Can they stay focused on the project?	☐ Yes	☐ No

If you got at least four yes answers, it may be fine to have your family assist with the organizing. If you answered three or more questions with no, then it may be best to work with them separately or give them homework assignments.

An example of homework would be small tasks like sorting through photos or paperwork in between your organizing sessions. These homework assignments help you get the tasks done that require your focused attention so we can do the more productive work during the in-person sessions.

How Long Do the Sessions Last?

I usually schedule organizing work for three to four hours per session. If we are doing a lot of emotional decision making, I recommend only three hours. If it is a garage clean-out or packing situation, we can work up to six or seven hours, but those jobs are usually done without the client. Most clients get overwhelmed after four hours, so we tackle the rest of the project another day.

Most often, the feeling of overwhelm that clients feel comes from emotional attachments, feelings of loss, and the idea that change is difficult even when it's a good change. When I begin to notice frustration in my clients halfway through the project, I remind them that it often gets harder before they begin to feel really good about things. I encourage them to press on and have patience so they can see the fruit of their labor and feel really great after the work is done.

What's in My Supply Bag?

I often refer to my organizing bag as "the Mary Poppins case." Although I have never pulled a lamp out of it, I would not be surprised to find one in the bottom. We always have: Post-its, Sharpie markers, labels and a super-duper label maker, Ziploc bags (all sizes), tape, rubber bands, scissors, a tape measure, and Command hooks. There is also a toolbox in my car because I need screwdrivers and hammers from time to time. Other items depend on each client's needs, such as moving boxes, storage bins, or over-the-door shoe holders. (There are dozens of uses for these handy storage items. Visit my website to see pictures of how you could use these space-saving items in each room of the house; www.SimplyOrganizedYou.com/Blog).

7

Should It Stay or Should It Go?

"Why the obsession with worldly possessions?
When it's your time to go, they have to stay behind,
so pack light."
~ Alex Morritt, Impromptu Scribe

Knowing what to expect from the organizing process can help relieve some of your anxiety.

The Simply Organized Process includes the following steps:

- Pull everything out.
- Put like with like.
- Pitch it.
- Give it away; give it away now.
- Decide what to keep.
- Relocate the MIAs.
- Find a home for everything.

Should It Stay or Should It Go?

My favorite phrase to hear during a client session is "Just make it go away!" Unfortunately, I don't hear this phrase from everyone. Most people have a difficult time making the decision to part with something. It's even harder when the item has sentimental value.

Our society is focused largely on obtaining things. People buy cars, houses, furniture, clothes, and electronics to feel good, to look good, and because it's fun. According to the movie The Story of Stuff, "Some reports indicate we consume twice as many material goods today as we did fifty years ago."[7] The result of all of this accumulation of stuff is clutter. If we don't get rid of some of it, it will take over our homes and our lives.

---

7 *The Story of Stuff.* Berkeley, CA: Free Range Studios, 2007. Accessed April 5, 2016. http://storyofstuff.org/

Not only does clutter invade your physical space, it can invade your mental space as well. A 2011 study by Princeton University's Neuroscience Institute reported that "Scientists find physical clutter negatively affects your ability to focus and process information."[8]

The obvious solution is to purge some of the unnecessary stuff. However, you have to know what you have before you can choose what to get rid of.

Step 1. Pull everything out.

The first step in the process is to pull everything out of the space you want organized. Once you get the items out of their old home, you can see them more clearly and decide what to do with them. For example, if we are organizing your kitchen, it's imperative to see all the pots and pans so we know how many you have, which ones you use, or if any are damaged.

Step 2. Put like with like.

Next begins the sorting process. Put all like items together. For example, if you are organizing a garage, group all rakes and shovels in one area, all tools together, and all auto-cleaning supplies in a separate spot.

Step 3. Pitch it.

Now it's time to get rid of what you can't use, what you don't need, or what you don't want. One of the easiest ways to tackle this is to start with the items that are broken,

---

8 Stephanie McMains and Sabine Kastner, "Interactions of Top-Down and Bottom-Up Mechanisms in Human Visual Cortex," *The Journal of Neuroscience,* January 12, 2011. Accessed April 5, 2016. http://www.jneurosci.org/content/31/2/587.long

are duplicates, or that have not been used and will not be used.

Examples of what to pitch:

- clothes with holes or stains
- soccer cleats that haven't been worn in eight years
- outfits you haven't been able to fit since middle school
- broken dishes
- your adult child's Smurf collection
- your adult child's textbooks
- everything in your home that belongs to your adult children (except photos)
- your adult child (or wait until the "give away" section)
- items you can't even identify
- anything with mold growing on it
- outdated technology (e.g., 8-track tapes and floppy computer disks)
- your tax files that are older than seven years

Step 4. Give it away; give it away now.

Donating to charities is the easiest and best way to get rid of items you no longer want or need while at the same time you are literally giving a gift to someone who really needs it! Many people want to know who is receiving their donated items. This creates a big road hump for you (another project or to-do on your list). Instead of taking your kid's clothes to your sister in Utah, your crock pot to your neighbor and your laptop to a high school, I'm asking you to relinquish those controlling thoughts and free yourself of any responsibilities. www.donationtown.org will show you a list of multiple charities who will pick up all of your items (including furniture) for free! The charities then sell those items to people in need and donate profits to charitable organizations. It is a WIN WIN WIN!!! There is even more information about donating in the next chapter.

Step 5. Decide what to keep.
Every person is different. You may have specific items that you must save, and that is okay. Each of those items can be included in your goals to ensure there is a plan to store, display, or maintain it. So what do you keep?

- what you need and use
- enough clothing so that you don't have to do laundry more than once per week
- one to two of each toiletry in the bathroom
- one set of dishes in the kitchen
- toys that your children still play with
- electronics that work and are used on a regular basis
- the things that make you happy
- photos and keepsakes that remind you of your family and friends
- anything you think of as part of your heart and soul

Gifts can present a problem. We all receive gifts we do not like or need. There is some sort of guilt associated with getting rid of a gift you've received. I call this "gift guilt." No one gives you a gift with the purpose of making you feel guilty (even after they have passed away). If the gift is never going to be used and is taking up space, regift it to a friend or donate it to a charity so they can either give it to someone who will enjoy it or so they can sell it as a fundraiser.

Ready to Release It?

To eliminate the overabundance of unwanted gifts, on future holidays, ask for gifts of service and time, such as home cleaning, babysitting your kids, dinner, concert tickets, four hours with an organizer (what a great idea), or gift certificates. Request these items from your friends and family and give these gifts instead of objects.

Remember this; everything is a balance. If you open a closet and stuff falls on your head, you have too much stuff. That does not mean you have to toss everything you own. It is a sign that it is time to pare down. If minimalism is your goal, I will help you achieve it, but my overall goal is for you to have less stress. That does not require getting rid of everything you own (just some of it).

Should It Stay or Should It Go?

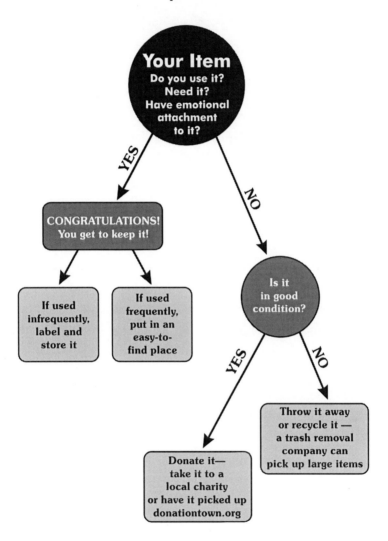

Remember Stacey? She had a secret stash of clothes hidden in her guest bedroom dresser and closets. As we tackled the task of downsizing her stash, she realized she never wore most of the clothing, so she decided to donate those items. In her living room, we reorganized her DVD storage, paring down which of those items to keep based on which ones she watched most. To help make her bill-paying process more efficient, we cleared her kitchen counters of excess mail and paperwork, used existing drawers and shelves in her dining area for storage, and then we created an organized bill-paying space. Now she knows what paperwork to keep and what to trash, rather than saving it all and watching the pile grow higher and higher in a space where it doesn't belong.

Step 6. Relocate the MIAs.

Where is the lid to that container? How did the other flip-flop get separated from this one? Your favorite red tie, where did you put it again? We all have items that get misplaced over time. Sometimes they're your favorites, and you mourn their absence. Sometimes you forget all about them, until they finally turn up in the most unlikely places. As you clear the problem areas of your home and office, misplaced items miraculously turn up. If they have a special meaning or use in your life, relocate them to the appropriate area and set up a system so they don't go MIA again.

Step 7. Find a home for everything.
Speaking of relocating items, you have to know that everything in your home has a place, even if that place is in the junk drawer. The most important thing is to decide where things belong. The second most important thing is to place items where they belong, every time, even when it seems inconvenient at the time. (You'll thank yourself later.) If you're a visual person, your space should be reorganized so items can be seen (key hanger near the door, clear bins, open shelving). On the other hand, if you don't wish to see items, but need to know where they are, label drawers, boxes, and bins as needed.

8

Give It Away;
Give It Away
Now

*"In the process of letting go
you will lose many things from the past,
but you will find yourself."*
~ *Deepak Chopra*

Reaching the point of deciding to eliminate items you've had for years is hard but liberating. There is a sense of release and calm, and for some, there's still a bit of anxiety associated with letting go of the stuff. But the result of having more space, more energy, better access to your stuff, and more control of your environment is well worth the sacrifice of giving up the items you don't need, use, or want.

Once you've decided to let your stuff go to a better place, the most obvious options are to resell it, donate it, trash it (which includes shredding), or recycle it.

Reselling

Many of my clients want to sell their unwanted items. Everything, including clothes, china, furniture, and collectibles, is very valuable to the people who spent a lot of their hard-earned money on it or received it from a loved one. Instead of considering the amount of money spent on the item when you purchased it brand new, realize that you have already received the value from your items during the time you've owned and used them. I hate to be the bearer of bad news, but these days, nothing is selling for as much as you would hope, and probably nowhere near as much as you paid for it. So keep this advice in mind when considering whether to resell your belongings. If it's not worth more than $50, think twice! It will cost you valuable hours of time posting it on Craigslist, Amazon, or eBay; screening buyers; and shipping your items.

If you're thinking about consigning clothes, expect to get $2 per piece of clothing, no matter what you paid for it or how good the condition of the item. I spent an entire day contacting children's clothing consignment stores, only to find that many of them weren't taking any new clothes at the time, and the ones that were required an appointment and only accepted twenty items per day. Your time is worth more than the items you're hoping to profit from.

If you are considering having a garage sale, consider instead having an estate sale or neighborhood-wide sale. With a garage sale, you can't control the weather on the day of your sale or the buyers who come, so you may wind up spending lots of time and not making very much money. However, neighborhood-wide sales and estate sales are advertised to a larger group of people, so they bring in more buyers and, hopefully, more money.

Estate sales are one of the easiest ways to get rid of many items you don't want or need, while also making some money. The way estate sales work is that you first hire an estate sale company that does all the work of pricing your items, publicizing the sale, handling the payments, and often arranging to have a hauling company available for customers who purchase large items and need them delivered. The estate sale company takes a percentage of the total sales. They also arrange to have a charity pick up all unsold items, and they provide a receipt for your tax records.

If you are staying in your home, I recommend an online estate sale company such as Max Sold or Everything But the House. This process is usually a win-win for all involved.

Donating

Donating unwanted treasures saves you lots of time. There are many organizations that make it easier than ever to donate, plus they bring trucks and a crew to do all the heavy lifting for you. You can drop off smaller items and clothing at Goodwill, the Humane Society Thrift Stores, the Salvation Army, and many more. If you have larger items, or just can't get around to dropping things off, call a pick-up service like the Veteran's Administration, the Kidney Foundation, the Humane Society, or a local charity. Many organizations donate profits and items from their thrift stores to abused women's charities. You get a tax deduction for your charitable donations, so you actually benefit in this area. The only catch is your items should be in decent condition. Nothing broken, no stains, and no rips. Also, most charities do not accept bedding, cribs, or car seats.

Trashing, Shredding, and Recycling

There are times when simply trashing items is the best thing to do, particularly when your stuff is well worn, damaged, or several years out of date (including furniture, appliances, technology, and clothing). In this case, trash removal companies will come to your home upon request and remove these items for you. They typically charge by the pound or load size.

For old paperwork and documents you no longer use or need, shredding is an excellent option, particularly when personal or other sensitive information is visible. Mobile shred trucks will shred documents on-site, or haul them away to shred later. As with trash companies, shredding companies typically charge by the pound or load size. You can also take your shred items to the UPS Store or any office supply store, where the cost is usually about $1 per pound for shredding documents.

Anything that has your Social Security number on it; any medical records; old tax documents (more than seven years old); and financial documents, such as bank, investment, and credit card statements, should be shredded. Do yourself and our environment a favor by signing up for electronic statements and online bill pay.

Many items can be recycled. You can place paper, aluminum and some plastic items into your home recycling bin. You probably have at least one old computer or a broken TV in your home; Best Buy customer service will recycle most electronics. For a list of the top ten most important items to recycle, go to: www.care2.com/causes /top-10-most-important-items-to-recycle.html.

Storage Units

Do you rent a storage unit? If so, you are not alone. About one in eleven American households rents a self-storage space and spends over $1,000 a year in rent.

According to the Self Storage Association, there are approximately 48,500 storage facilities in the United States. Americans spent more than $27 billion to store our stuff in 2014, helping make the self-storage industry among the fastest growing business sectors for the past forty years.[9] To put this into perspective, *Reader's Digest* reports that, "You

---

9 Self Storage Association. Accessed April 5, 2016. http://www.selfstorage.org/ LinkClick.aspx?fileticket=fJYAow6_AU0%3D&portalid=0

could buy all the stuff in your storage unit for the price of the annual rental fee, and that doesn't include the cost of the moving truck."[10]

Storage pods like Smart Box are a great temporary option for storing items. This type of storage saves the need for multiple moves by storing your boxes and then delivering them to your new home. These mobile storage boxes can come in handy when you are moving and can't get into your new place yet, you have a finite period of time to store your things, such as sixty days, or you are remodeling your home and need to get certain items out of the way.

6 Reasons to Use Storage Containers for Short-term Storage

Clutter can be a headache. It's an eyesore and it drains you mentally. Whether your clutter is inside your home, in your garage, or stored in a backyard shed, it's likely taking up space that could be better used for something else. But who has time to drag all that stuff to a far-off storage facility?

That's where SMARTBOX comes in. SMARTBOX storage containers provide convenient, affordable storage, delivered directly to your door, so you can easily place the clutter in a storage container and create the clutter-free space you've been dreaming of.

---

10 Michelle Crouch, "13+ Secrets Personal Organizers Would Never Tell You For Free," *The Reader's Digest*. Accessed April 5, 2016. http://www.rd.com/home/cleaning-organizing/personal-organizers-secrets-free/

So when is a good time to use SMARTBOX storage containers?

1. **Home staging:** When staging your home for sale, store excessive furniture and decor to keep each room clutter free.
2. **Moving:** Have a SMARTBOX storage container delivered to your home and load it easily at your own pace. Then, have it moved to your climate controlled SMARTBOX facility later.
3. **House guests:** Need to clear out that guest room that has somehow become the store-all space? Clear it out to make room for holiday guests.
4. **Renovations:** Now you have a safe space to store your furniture during home renovations.
5. **College students:** Gone for a semester or two? Turn your college student's room into the office or workout room you've been wanting. Store his or her items in a SMARTBOX container temporarily.
6. **Additional vehicle:** Clear your garage of excess tools or sporting equipment so you can park your new or additional vehicle.

SMARTBOX offers an array of storage options. Visit www.SmartBoxMovingAndStorage.com to learn about our smart storage solutions to help conquer your clutter.

Downsizing Debbie

When I met Debbie, I knew immediately we were going to be friends. She is the coolest senior citizen I have ever known. (Sorry, Mom and Dad.) She hired me to declutter her home to get ready for a move from a 2,000-square-foot home into a 600-square-foot apartment at an independent living facility. Debbie knew she had too much stuff. She was very motivated to part with clothing (she donated more than forty bags), but kept getting stuck on holiday decorations, her beloved Atlanta Falcons memorabilia, and tailgating items.

We pared her stuff down enough to fit comfortably in her new apartment, but she insisted on renting not one but two storage units! I fought her with every rational statistic I had, but she could not part with anything else, so I gave in, satisfied that we had at least helped her accomplish a successful move. After I got her settled, I continued to follow up with her regularly to see if she needed help.

Update*: After living in her new place for a year, Debbie finally called me to help her get rid of the storage units, which she had not been to since the movers filled them up the year prior. We donated two units full of great stuff, for which Debbie received a charitable tax deduction. She is no longer saddled with a monthly rental fee, and most importantly, she is free of the guilt and anxiety the excess items were causing her. You can't put a price on that! To find out how much money Debbie wasted on storage rental and movers, go to page 126.*

Self-storage units can become the point of no return. Most times, the stuff you store there will never return to your home, and you get absolutely no return on the investment you make to store your items.

4 Reasons Long-term Storage is a No-win Option

1 Items put into storage units are never seen again. If an out-of-sight item is likely to become out of mind, get rid of it sooner rather than later.

2 The cost for the monthly rental on the unit, in addition to the time and cost needed to move the items into storage, end up being a huge waste. Instead, invest your time in regularly maintaining structure and calm in your surroundings, and invest your money in trips or activities that create memories with family and friends.

3 Many items put into storage are never used, hence they were chosen to go to storage instead of remaining in your home. If you are not using it, let it go.

4 The reasons items go to storage are usually based on gift guilt, buyer's remorse, or holding on to stuff for your children or relatives to have in the future. If you think your children would want the items later, ask them before you pay for storage, then give the stuff to your children now.

9

The
Glue

*"You wouldn't train for a marathon and then
give up a mile before the finish line.
Same goes with your life and dreams."*
~ Dawn Gluskin

This is the best part! You have made all the difficult decisions, you have space in your home, and now you can put everything back where it belongs. Here's where you get to see the magic happen, when everything comes together and you can breathe.

Every item should have its own home. During a TV appearance, Peter Walsh, professional organizer extraordinaire, shared that everyone has a place in their house for forks. If you found a random fork in the bathroom or under the couch, you'd immediately know it didn't belong there and would return it to its drawer without another thought. Everything in your life should be this easy to put away, he stated. If an item occupies no specific location when it's not in use, it becomes clutter. If every item has a permanent place, then it never gets lost and every person in your family knows exactly where it goes every time.

Revisit your goals to determine if you're still on track. Have any of your goals changed? It's perfectly fine if they have. This whole process is about working through and accepting change. Maybe you need to tweak your filing system because you can't find something, or you may want to move the snacks in the pantry so the kids can reach them more easily (or move them higher so they won't eat them and ruin their appetites for dinner). This goal-reassessment process helps you move forward.

If you are constantly losing your keys, cell phone, homework, bills, shoes, wallet, or other items, the goal is to find a place for those items and create a system to help you put them there every day when you get home or every night before you go to bed. Have your children and spouse or partner get in to the same habit. There should be a five-minute quick clean each evening, during which all items out of place get put into their homes. This is a huge time savings, especially for the hectic mornings most families experience.

The Drop Zone

Creating a personalized system means your items and their homes make the most sense for you and your family. If you're like most people, having a drop zone creates the perfect space for mail, bills, and other items. The mudroom is the perfect place. If you don't have a mudroom, there is likely some other space in your home that would work. This should be near the entrance and exit door you use most.

Your drop zone is the place for things you need to quickly access, such as the items below:

- incoming mail
- backpacks or briefcases and purses
- a charging station for your cell phones and laptops
- a calendar or bulletin board for important reminders and messages your family will see quickly

The Action Center

People tend to pile papers and mail on countertops and tabletops. Instead, a vertical hanging file holder works better to place mail in. This is your action center. Have a slot for ASAP/VIP, labeled "DAILY," a slot for bills to pay, labeled "WEEKLY," and another slot for papers to file, labeled "MONTHLY." Also, have a trashcan or shredder for the junk mail that should be tossed right away. Set a reminder and alarm on your phone to empty your slots at the same time each day, week, and month. This way nothing piles up, and you won't be overwhelmed by paper. Some clients like to have a paper holder or slot for each family member or for kids' school papers (except home-work, which should stay in their backpacks).

Systemizing the Smiths

Gabe and Amanda Smith needed help coming up with new systems. A young married couple, it seemed they'd had everything go wrong. They lost their jobs, they lost their house, and their parents were very sick. Amanda had health issues herself and had taken a work-from-home job to make ends meet. Gabe was still on the job hunt and taking any odd job that came his way when they came to me in total desperation to get their house in order so they could work from home and gain some sense of peace in their stressful lives.

Each room of their rental home was filled with items to unpack or get rid of, and there was no space to put anything else. I began by making one room a total Zen experience. The goal was to tackle Amanda's home office first, then Gabe's office, while also keeping their dining room, living room, and master bedroom in mind as part of the entire project. They did not have a big budget, nor did they have a lot of time to work.

After removing furniture and other items from their sunroom, we designated what was to be donated or sold online and what would be taken to their backyard storage shed, which was eventually converted into a beautiful space for them to exercise and relax.

As we continued the process of putting things back together, we tackled Amanda's boxes of paperwork in her office and rearranged furniture to create various areas for work, crafts, and supply storage. The excess papers were either filed or shredded.

Understandably, Gabe and Amanda had gotten behind on a lot of their bills. To solve this issue, we created a system using vertical hanging file holders placed on the front of each of their office doors and labeled "VIP" (for RSVPs and urgent bills to look at and clear out daily), "To Pay" (to be handled weekly), and "To File" (to be emptied monthly). We set alarms on their calendars for the same time each day, week, and month for these tasks to be completed.

With these systems in place, both Gabe and Amanda were noticeably relieved when we completed their home reorganizing project, and I could tell they were beginning to have a new lease on life.

Update: The Smiths are maintaining the systems we put in place, and with the clutter cleared from their home and minds, it seems their luck is taking a turn for the better. I'm amazed at their positive attitudes and motivation. Even though horrible things kept happening to them, they did not let those events get them down. They simply needed someone with the life skills to teach them how to get their daily tasks and space back in order.

Now that you have your systems in place and all of your items in their homes, it's time to look at maintaining this newly organized household of yours.

10

Keep On
Keepin' On

"Energy and persistence
conquer all things."
~ Benjamin Franklin

What? You're not done? Sorry to say it, but remember that elbow grease and time mentioned earlier? That never ends. The process does, however, get much easier now that you have the groundwork set up. Your systems may not be working for you. Your family may not be helping with quick cleans and evening prep work. You may have a set-back, like an injury or illness. No matter the reason, don't think of it as a failure. Maintenance is about consistency and fixing what is not working.

Have you ever worked out for many months or years and then just stopped? When you get started again, your muscles have memories of the exercise you did in the past, so it's easier to get back on the horse. Remember your life is just like laundry; you are never finished (unless you're a nudist). The most important thing is to notice very early when your space needs attention and do something about it. It will be much easier to get organized this time, especially since you don't have as much stuff to get rid of.

I left Stacey with a well-organized home after working with her for a little over a year. I still check in with her from time to time to ensure the systems are working for her. The systems we put into place for her are working great in her library, kitchen, bedroom, den, and laundry room. The area she's been frustrated with is her mail and paperwork. I

love that she reaches out to me for help with maintenance before things get too bad.

One system doesn't work for everyone. What works for Stacey are dedicated bins. We call this an action center. To help with her paperwork, we set up one bin for weekly items like mail, bills to pay, RSVPs, and credit cards. The second bin is for monthly items, such as papers to file, tax documents, and medical and insurance papers. With the alarms set for her to check the bins at regular intervals, Stacey can maintain this system easily.

Clutter can be a never-ending nemesis. Even with the automatic and electronic resources at your disposal, modern life still includes items that can build up and eventually become clutter. Here are some tips to keep clutter at bay:

- Every day, go through your mail immediately. Throw away the junk, and place your bills and other items in an organized space. Have a mail action center where you place ASAP, weekly, and monthly file folders, and handle them in a timely fashion. Set an alarm on your calendar to remind you to empty the folders.
- Tackle your space regularly. Spend a dedicated hour per month or fifteen minutes per week decluttering and putting things where they belong.
- When you shop, take a list and don't stray from it. Only buy what you need.

- If someone gives you something you don't need or want, donate or regift it immediately, or ask for the receipt and take it back.
- Don't go to garage sales or antique stores or order from those late-night infomercials. Whatever your purchasing trigger is, avoid it.
- If you feel sad or lonely, meet a friend for coffee or take a walk instead of shopping.
- Get some accountability. Most organizers offer a follow-up service. They will call you on a regular basis to check in and see how you are doing. Some clients like us to give homework so they can achieve a few tasks every month on their own. If you experience a major life change, like moving, illness, or divorce, contact us so we can alter your systems to make them work better.

Time Management

Maintenance is not only about keeping your stuff organized; it also includes time management. If you lead a hectic life, it helps to have someone from outside your family guide you and help you figure out where you can save some time and focus your energy more effectively. Perhaps you need to set daily tasks and alarms so your regular activities become routine. You might also need someone to follow up with you on a weekly basis to ensure you're staying on top of your assignments and keeping up with your calendar, emails, and voicemails. When you're in the midst of juggling a long workweek, family, social engagements, health, and maybe studying for an important test, it's important to plan ahead, block off enough time, and look at your calendar every day so you don't forget anything. When things like paperwork start to slip through the cracks, it's important to look at each day, week, month, and year as a whole to get back on track.

Here are a few time management and self-care tips to help you maintain peace of mind and gain control of your time:

- Focus on one thing at a time and complete that task. (Remember multitasking is a distraction.)
- If you must multitask, do only one physical and one mental task at a time. For example, you can talk on the phone and fold laundry, but I strongly recommend you do not talk on the phone and email at the same time.
- Set reasonable and attainable goals for yourself and your family. If you are making a daily to-do list, only place three to five items per day on the list. Prioritize them to ensure the most important item on the list is first so that will definitely get done.
- Block off entire chunks of time on your calendar instead of just the time of your appointment or task. Make sure to include drive time. If your doctor's appointment is at noon, your calendar should state 10:30 a.m. to 2:00 p.m. to include traffic and wait time.
- Do not procrastinate. Set a twenty-minute timer, put on your favorite music, put your phone away, and just do it. The more you put the task off, the more stress it will cause you.

- Do not overcommit. It's okay to say no. If you overextend yourself, you can't give one hundred percent to anything. You're actually doing everyone a favor by choosing to give your time and energy only when you have it to give. Every time you say yes to one person or opportunity, you are saying no to someone or something else. Value your own time and others will too.

Here are several ways to save time in the hectic morning hours:

- Get your clothes out the night before. Have your kids gets their clothes ready too.
- Let kids prep breakfast and lunches the night before.
- Set up an entryway drop zone where all purses and backpacks are kept. You may also choose to keep shoes here and use this space as a charging station where your cell phones and tablets go each night to be charged. This is a great place for your family calendar (if you like a printed or dry-erase version). Put your keys here, on hooks or in a bowl, every time you come in the door. Once you do this, you will no longer spend your mornings looking for your stuff.
- Set up a carpool with your neighbors or parents whose children share your children's activities. Carpooling two to three days per week (to school, sports, and entertainment venues) could save you six to ten hours per week of drive time.

- Try to get a couple of errands done on your way to work or school or on your way home.
- Get your prescriptions refilled where you buy your groceries. This saves gas money and helps ensure you don't forget anything.
- Keep your to-do lists in your car so you can check off items each day. Whether you use your phone or a notepad, keep the list handy so you can update it and use it when needed.
- Plan your meals every week and make a grocery list based on your weekly menu. This saves time and money. You only go to the store once per week, and you don't have to think of what's for dinner each day when you get home.
- Cook several meals at once and freeze them so you don't have to cook every night.
- Use the slow cooker while you're away all day.

Purchase a 25-page Weekly Menu and Grocery List tear-off pad with magnet for your fridge: www.SimplyOrganizedYou.com/Resources

Grocery List

VEGETABLES
- ○ Lettuce
- ○ Tomatoes
- ○ Carrots
- ○ Cucumbers
- ○ Garlic
- ○ Peppers
- ○ Onions
- ○ Potatoes
- ○ Broccoli
- ○ Mushrooms
- ○ ....
- ○ ....
- ○ ....

FRUIT
- ○ Bananas
- ○ Apples
- ○ Oranges
- ○ Grapes
- ○ Melons
- ○ Berries
- ○ ....
- ○ ....
- ○ ....

CANNED
- ○ Beans
- ○ Fruit
- ○ Soup
- ○ Vegetables
- ○ Tuna Fish
- ○ Tomato Sauce
- ○ ....
- ○ ....
- ○ ....

SAUCES
- ○ Oil
- ○ Vinegar
- ○ Salad Dressing
- ○ Pasta Sauce
- ○ ....
- ○ ....
- ○ ....

DRY GOODS
- ○ Bread
- ○ Pasta
- ○ Cereal
- ○ Rice
- ○ Tortillas
- ○ Muffins
- ○ Bagels
- ○ ....
- ○ ....
- ○ ....

SNACKS
- ○ Chips
- ○ Pretzels
- ○ Cookies
- ○ Crackers
- ○ Nuts
- ○ Popcorn
- ○ Snack Bars
- ○ Candy
- ○ ....
- ○ ....
- ○ ....

MEAT & FISH
- ○ Beef
- ○ Poultry
- ○ Pork
- ○ Fish
- ○ Bacon
- ○ Sausage
- ○ Deli Meat
- ○ ....
- ○ ....
- ○ ....

BAKING
- ○ Sugar
- ○ Flour
- ○ Baking Powder
- ○ Spices
- ○ ....
- ○ ....
- ○ ....

DAIRY
- ○ Milk
- ○ Butter
- ○ Eggs
- ○ Cheese
- ○ Yogurt
- ○ ....
- ○ ....
- ○ ....

FROZEN
- ○ Pizza
- ○ Meals
- ○ Vegetables
- ○ Ice Cream
- ○ ....
- ○ ....
- ○ ....

BEVERAGES
- ○ Water
- ○ Juice
- ○ Soda
- ○ Coffee
- ○ Tea
- ○ ....
- ○ ....
- ○ ....

HOUSEHOLD
- ○ Paper Towels
- ○ Toilet Paper
- ○ Tissues
- ○ Garbage Bags
- ○ Plastic Bags
- ○ Laundry Soap
- ○ Dish Soap
- ○ Cleaner
- ○ Sponges
- ○ Batteries
- ○ Light Bulbs
- ○ Aluminum Foil
- ○ ....
- ○ ....
- ○ ....

CONDIMENTS
- ○ Peanut Butter
- ○ Jelly
- ○ Honey
- ○ Mayonnaise
- ○ Mustard
- ○ Catsup
- ○ Pickles
- ○ ....
- ○ ....
- ○ ....

TOILETRIES
- ○ Shampoo
- ○ Conditioner
- ○ Razor
- ○ Deodorant
- ○ Lotion
- ○ Toothpaste
- ○ Hand Soap
- ○ ....
- ○ ....
- ○ ....

PETS
- ○ Dog Food
- ○ Cat Food
- ○ Litter
- ○ ....
- ○ ....
- ○ ....

REMEMBER
- ○ ....
- ○ ....
- ○ ....
- ○ ....
- ○ ....
- ○ ....
- ○ ....
- ○ ....
- ○ ....
- ○ ....
- ○ ....
- ○ ....

Routine

Kids (and adults) thrive on routines. Knowing what your daily, weekly, and monthly schedules look like is comforting. If you have routines set, you experience less confusion and fewer communication issues. You and your family know what to expect, and as a result, you experience less chaos. Even if you have multiple weekly activities, like sports, that take you away from home some evenings, keep the routines intact for when the family is home. This sets clear expectations and healthy habits for the whole family.

Sample Daily Schedule

Time	Activity
6:30 AM	Wake up, get dressed
7:00 AM	Breakfast, brush teeth
7:30 AM	Arrive at bus (drive to work)
8:00 AM – 3:00 PM	School/work
3:00 – 4:00 PM	Homework
4:00 – 5:00 PM	Play
5:00 – 6:00 PM	Chores/prep for next day (clothes laid out, snacks and lunches made, set table for dinner, etc.)
6:00 – 7:00 PM	Dinner
7:00 – 7:30 PM	Bath time
7:30 – 8:00 PM	Read stories
8:00 PM	Bedtime

Download a blank Daily Schedule at:
www.SimplyOrganizedYou.com/Resources.

Of course, you will want to tweak your family's routine slightly during the weekends. Don't change the bedtime and wake-up time too much, or you'll pay for it on Monday morning. Make sure you have a monthly family meeting to get everyone's activities on a calendar. Whether you like a dry-erase or printed calendar, or prefer an online shared one, each family member should have their own color. This makes it much easier to see what each person has scheduled each day.

Lastly, make time for yourself. We all spend too much time doing for everyone else, and then we feel burned out and resentful. To gain more energy in your life, carve out some time for just you. Take a walk, hire a sitter, get a massage, go out with friends, or turn off your phone and just enjoy silence for a few minutes each day.

Time management and routine play a big part at work too. For my business clients, I help their staff stay on task. There are many tools and apps you can use for to-do lists, task management, online calendars, and staying motivated. Some, such as the following, are very simple to use and don't cost a dime:

- Your smart phone calendar, plus alarms and reminders
- Evernote: task manager
- Unroll.me: by far, my favorite way to control email
- Due: sets timers for chores or tasks
- EpicWin: a game that gives you points for accomplishing real-life tasks

You might also need help setting both short-term and long-term goals. These can include goals as simple as showing up on time (not so simple for some), or as complex as studying for and passing an exam. The key is to find a system and tools that work for you. Not everyone embraces technology, so if a paper calendar works for you, keep using a paper calendar. If it will take twenty-plus hours to learn a new system, then go with an easier one.

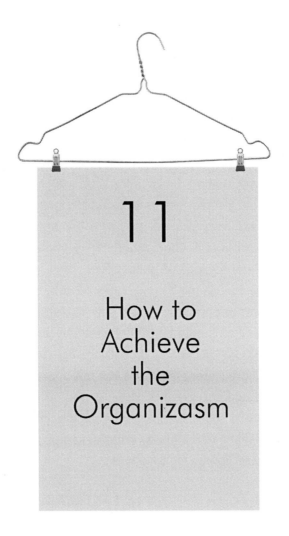

11

How to
Achieve
the
Organizasm

"The leader is one who, out of the clutter,
brings simplicity . . . out of discord, harmony . . .
and out of difficulty, opportunity."
~ Albert Einstein

This is the part where you get to breathe a sigh of relief. You have crossed the finish line, and it's time to collect your prize. This is what I call the "organizasm," a silly word I made up to describe the wonderful feeling of getting organized. Consider looking at a before photo to remind yourself of where you were, how much you've accomplished, and what your new space looks like. This is the time to pat yourself on the back for a job well done!

Like some people, you may wonder if you'll ever miss the items you've gotten rid of. For most people, the joy experienced through the organizing process seems to overpower any feelings of guilt or loss. With your organization projects complete, you'll get to fully enjoy your home. More importantly, you'll get to enjoy your life because you'll no longer be overwhelmed by your stuff.

There is no magic to organizing. Spending lots of money on storage containers will not make you organized. The organizing fairy does not come to your home and do it for you. It takes some special planning, time, elbow grease, and maintenance to make any organizing project a success. And the results can be life transforming!

What You Can Expect to *Feel* When You Are Done

Free. The feeling of freedom comes when all of the clutter and confusion have been taken away. You gain more time in your life, and are free to do something other than worry about not being organized.

Happy. You can find everything you need, when you need it, which makes you very happy. You find yourself smiling when you enter your home now.

Proud and accomplished. You have achieved greatness! You want to show your beautiful home to all of your neighbors and friends.

Relieved. When you walk into your home, there is no longer dread or stress, just relief that your project is done.

Light. Now that you've removed probably hundreds of pounds of the stuff that was weighing you down, you feel lighter. You have no excess baggage or weight—just lightness.

Motivated. You tackled your organizing project; what's next? The positive feelings you experience after achieving a goal make you want to do more. You can take on anything now!

Like a winner. Your home is an organized space, and you did it! You conquered the dragon and won the race.

What You'll Reclaim When You Are Done

Time. You no longer waste precious time looking for stuff that is lost. This helps you focus on the things that bring you joy and also helps you arrive on time (or even early, imagine that!) to important events and meetings.

Energy. That physical clutter had turned into emotional clutter that was draining you. Now you have energy to do what you love with the people you love.

Control. It's all back in your hands. You have conquered your space issues, and now you control what your home and life look like. You made the tough decisions, and now you can do anything you want.

Here are some comments we've received from our clients when we completed their organizing projects:

"I didn't know how much this would change my life for the better."

"We don't have to hide our stuff before a party anymore."

"I invited my friends over for the first time ever!"

"You saved our marriage."

"I'm starting an organizing business so I can help others the way you've helped me."

See more client testimonials on our website: www.SimplyOrganizedYou.com/Testimonials.

Grieving Gretta

My client Gretta was going through many life changes at once. Gretta was a young widow and needed help getting her suburban home ready to sell. Her children were all grown up and had moved out, and she was ready to move into a smaller place. Gretta was ready to part with a lot of items, which made our work with her easy.

During our sessions, we sorted through her belongings and categorized them to keep or take, purge or sell. All unwanted items were put in storage, and items in good condition that she didn't want were decluttered, cleaned, and prepared to sell during an estate sale. We helped her hire movers, rent storage units (only for two months), hire an estate sale company, stage her home, pack, and unpack. The estate sale, which occurred during the thirty-day closing period, was a huge success.

Update: About two weeks after she sold her home, Gretta called to tell me she had been laid off from her job of more than twenty years. Although disappointed, she said that, after working with me, she felt so light and stress free that she wanted to help others feel the same way. Instead of looking at her job loss as a negative, she saw it as an opportunity to start her own business (to see what kind of business, go to page 126). She asked if I would be her mentor and assist her while she got her business up and running. I happily agreed, and I'm proud to say that Gretta is doing very well.

12

Stick A
Fork In Me;
I'm Done

*"You may never know what results come
of your actions, but if you do nothing,
there will be no results."*
~ Mahatma Gandhi

Now that you've read this book, you know what it takes (and doesn't take) to achieve order and calm so you can reclaim time, energy, and control of your life.

Remember this:

- Your home, office, or life didn't become cluttered overnight, and it won't get decluttered overnight. The organizing fairy does not come to your home and do it for you. It takes planning, time, elbow grease, and maintenance to make any organizing project a success.
- Being disorganized costs you time, money, efficiency, and peace of mind. But you can change all of this for the better.
- There is no magic to organizing. Spending lots of money on containers will not make you organized.
- It's okay to ask for help.
- Professional organizers are skilled at what they do. (Some are specialists.) Their goal is to help you achieve your goal, not to throw away all of your stuff or make you feel bad, guilty, or ashamed.
- Setting goals and expectations at the start of your organizing project is essential to achieving success and results.
- There is a process to organizing your life (home, work, time, etc.) that includes setting up systems you can easily maintain.
- Accountability is important in the organizing process.
- When you're ready to release the clutter, an organizer can help make it go away.

- Maintaining a simple, organized life takes commitment and systems, and sometimes you need help with that.

Hopefully you were able to find at least one story (if not more) in this book to relate to. You may not be going through any major life changes right now, but you may still feel disorganized (in other words, you are human). Or maybe your life has been touched by marriage, death, divorce, physical or mental illness, or a move, and you now know that these life changes do not have to result in clutter and confusion. Write down your goals and give yourself a deadline to achieve them. Remember that a positive attitude goes a long way towards achieving your goals.

You Can Do This!

But you don't have to do it alone. Professional organizers, like me, have resources to help you; all you have to do is ask.

If you want your home to be the relaxing, comfortable space you've always dreamed of, call us. If you want to stop worrying about the errands, appointments, work, shopping, cooking, and cleaning, send me an email. If you want to stress less and spend more time doing what you love with who you love, we are here when you need us!

No matter where you live, you can get help from Simply Organized. We offer online organizing classes for both residential and office organization, as well as time-management coaching. Please see our website for more information.

Simply Organized | www.SimplyOrganizedYou.com
404.825.2105 | heather@SimplyOrganizedYou.com

Simply Organized Tips

Managing Paperwork

- Open incoming mail daily, and review bills and action items weekly.
- Keep a separate, visible, easily accessible folder or bin for each.

Kids and Homework

- Create color-coded file folders for each school subject.
- Keep all to-do work on the left side of the folder, and move it to the right side when it's completed.
- Each night before bed, make sure all homework is in backpacks and all items in the drop zone for the next morning. Same for files and supplies needed for work the next day.

Moving

- Prior to packing, discard (trash or donate) all items that are damaged or outdated or that are too large or not useful in your new space.
- Prepare your home for showing by staging each room to clearly illustrate one specific use.
- Depersonalize your home to make it more attractive to prospective buyers so they can imagine their

family living there. (Remove all photos, awards, and sports memorabilia.)

Meals and Grocery Shopping

- Use the slow cooker to cook meals while you're away during the day so dinner is ready when you arrive home.
- Package leftovers in small containers that can be easily packed for lunch the next day.
- Use a grocery list organized by the aisle in which items are found in the store to avoid forgetting items on your list. Purchase your own Weekly Menu and Grocery List pad at www.SimplyOrganizedYou.com /Resources.

Housework and Chores

- Create a chore chart with color coding for each child or family member's daily or weekly responsibilities. Place it on the refrigerator with days each chore should be completed.
- Clean one room per day to maintain clean areas without spending an entire day cleaning.
- Select one day to do laundry for the week, and complete the entire task (wash, dry, fold, put away).

Closets (clothes, linens, medicine)

- Organize clothes on closet racks by type (pants, tops, etc.) and color (for each type of clothing).
- After folding, place sheets (fitted and top) inside one pillowcase to keep matching sets together.

- Store daily medications in a visible place for easy accessibility. Less-used medicines (cold, allergy) and emergency items (bandages, antiseptic) or supplies (tweezers, thermometer) can be stored separately.

Visit www.SimplyOrganizedYou.com/Blog for more useful tips.

Resources

Websites

- www.ThredUp.com (resell clothing)
- www.Unroll.me (unsubscribe to all unwanted emails or get one email per day)
- www.parents.com (chore charts and meal planners)
- Donations: www.donationtown.org
- Carbonite.com (computer backup)

Apps

- Key Ring: keep all rewards cards in one place
- 1Password: keep all your passwords in one place (and only have to remember one)
- Doctor on Demand: 24/7 access to physicians
- Groove Book: print photos from your devices
- Hootsuite: manage all social media in one place
- Due: set timers for your chores
- Evernote: for notes and to-do lists
- EpicWin: rewards completed chores with points earned

Favorite Products in Stores

- Real Simple hanging storage organizers (Bed Bath and Beyond)
- Space Bags (www.spacebag.com or retail stores)

- Ozone machine: rent at any party or tool rental supply company
- Sterilite Stack and Carry
- Post-it notes
- Sharpie markers
- Command hooks
- Ziploc bags
- Grab Bags
- Non-slip hangers
- Plastic envelopes (for coupons)
- Accordion files (for taxes)
- Clear plastic bins for storage (all sizes)

Online

- Jokari gift bag hanging organizer
- Whitmor gift wrap hanging organizer
- ClosetMaid Pantry over-the-door rack

Resources for Help with ADD

- www.helpguide.org/articles/add-adhd/adult-adhd-attention-deficit-disorder-self-help.htm#organization

The Answers You've Been Looking For

Stella (Chapter 1)

Stella's Steiff teddy bear collection included 522 cute, cuddly little bears. She was brave enough to part with about 400 of them before the move, but brought a total of 100 with her to her new apartment.

Dan (Chapter 3)

We all need a chair to sit on, but did Dan really need nearly 175? That's how many chairs he had collected over the years. He donated a few and put some up for resale, but he took 26 with him to his new apartment. At least he'll have plenty of seating for guests!

Sally (Chapter 5)

Between Sally and her six daughters, they donated 1,956 dresses to a charity. Over the years, the girls had grown and changed sizes several times, plus many of the dresses were outdated.

Tina (Chapter 5)

The only client to date who has requested we relocate an item previously donated was Tina, and this wasn't due to any emotional attachment she had to it. Once our work was done, she realized she needed space to store her books. She remembered there was a bookshelf she donated that would be the perfect space. So we retrieved it and helped Tina organize her books.

Debbie (Chapter 8)

Debbie realized that she had wasted $1,440 on monthly rental fees, plus about $400 for the movers.

Gretta (Chapter 11)

You probably guessed it. Gretta started her own professional organizing business! She wanted to help others as much as she was helped working with us.

About The Author

Heather Rogers is a professional organizer and owner of Simply Organized. She and her team specialize in helping people decrease the clutter in their lives, create a more organized environment, manage their time more effectively, and maintain calm in the midst of a busy life. Her clients include professionals and entrepreneurs who work from home, anyone who is getting their home ready to sell, individuals and families who need help packing or unpacking, and busy professionals and families who need assistance with time management and space maintenance coaching.

A Georgia native, Heather has worked in the insurance and financial services industries, as well as in customer service and sales. She has a passion for helping people and a keen sense of spatial planning and organizing. Ironically, she earned a bachelor's degree in risk management from the University of Georgia. (Isn't being disorganized one of the greatest risks in life?) She is Director of Professional Development for the Georgia Chapter of the National Association of Professional Organizers (NAPO) and frequently speaks to groups about the benefits of time management and the costs of disorganization.

At Simply Organized, she manages a team of professionals who understand that being organized is an ongoing process for even the most organized people.

Heather addresses the emotional issues and causes of disorganization to help clients achieve a happy and peaceful home, family life, and work environment to help make life easier. The reassurance she gives her clients is simply put: "I've got this—let me take the wheel!"

Heather lives near Atlanta, Georgia, with her husband, Tim, and their dog, Sophie.